Amores

Poems of Bernard Filipow

BERNARD FILIPOW

Amores
Copyright © 2022 by Bernard Filipow

All rights reserved. No part of this publication may be reproduced,
distributed, or transmitted in any form or by any means, including
photocopying, recording, or other electronic or mechanical
methods, without the prior written permission of the author, except
in the case of brief quotations embodied in critical reviews and
certain other non-commercial uses permitted by copyright law.

Tellwell Talent
www.tellwell.ca

ISBN
978-0-2288-7614-4 (Hardcover)
978-0-2288-7612-0 (Paperback)
978-0-2288-7613-7 (eBook)

To my sister, Sandra...
and in memory of our
uncle, Gino Spironello.

Books by Bernard Filipow

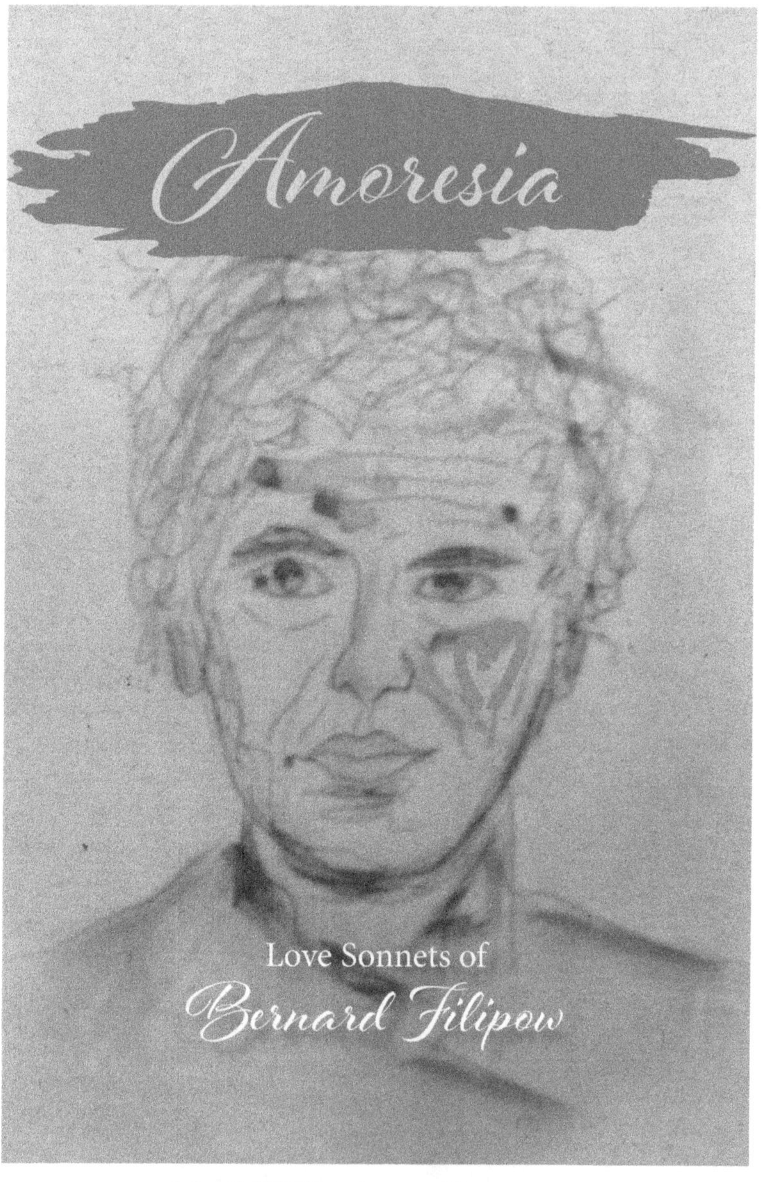

AMORESIA Love Sonnets

THE BLUE TORTOISE

TORTOISE
青いカメ

HAIKU POEMS
by
BERNARD FILIPOW

THE BLUE TORTOISE Haiku Poems

The Poems

Diurnal migrant to my love must bring
A melodious message this early spring
And to your own voice you must be true
Though others may try to imitate you
A love song of devotion in display flight
At break of day rising or early night
To weld our lonely hearts as one
That we may rejoice in the eternal sun.
If in all this you will succeed,
Your mission will honour love's deed.

Memories persist
In the fragrance of a rose
Of her beauty blessed.

Spring loves in winter
Where tender thoughts still linger
Of what might have been.

My name was a name
Until I heard her say it
Then it became hers.

Can there be such love?
I, attached as your shadow
Blue in the noon sun.

Caressed by her eyes
And touched by her divine hands
He painted a love.

Like the zephyrs through your boughs
doth blow,
Gentle waves that ever ebb and flow,
On my heart, your love the breeze bestow
An arrow sent from Cupid's fateful bow.
How tenderly were our hearts combined,
Trapped in the mysteries of spring love,
As in a net of thee were we entwined,
Unaware of ominous clouds above.
When love comes early, the fates intervene,
Summoning all the doubts and the fears
And the hurt that may come in between,
"So regretful!" E'en after all these years.
That I knew then what I know now,
My ever weeping love, Lau Siu Lau.

From his heart to hers
Love letters written in ink
On "cotton" paper.

Face wrinkled and grey
Her heart tender and open
Ever seeking love.

A single kiss blown to a lonely doe,
Elegantly, as Glam Cherie don't you
know!

At dusk, appears the firefly
In synchronistic luminescence
Nature's pyrotechnic display in
July
FIlled with the hope of romance.

"Could we love were we to live forever?"
"Would romantic feelings be as intense?"
"Would the hearts of lovers be as tender?"
"Would loving anyone at all make sense?"
Alas time would not be as precious
Nor as fleeting as the wandering moon,
Nor lovers' entreaties compendious,
Nor could a love affair be o'r too soon.
"Does ephemeral time fan lovers hearts
Knowing the flames will not last forever,
Stoking the fire impassioned love imparts
That welds their adoring hearts together?
And, does this love extend beyond time?"
This would be "unquestionably" sublime.

How foolish was I to ignore our love
And not realize how rare a treasure,
Now I question the heavens above
For the lives we could have shared together.
'Tis perplexing why I still lament so-
'Twas over half a century ago.

It only comes once
The love that outlives starlight
Once in a lifetime.

Penniless in love
With no gift to buy favour
My gift was my verse.

Blown off course
By the winds of his libido
And the swells of his inflated ego.
Of the fine he had to pay
Little did he ever say.
And all for a brief moment of bliss
While lost in a lane lover's unholy kiss.

A knock on the window
The stunned catbird ascending
A grieving lover's reprieve.

My heart is a bird
In a gilded cage singing
Of migrating winds.

In the hurtful denouement of romance,
Love quickly melts away as "cire perdue",
For no reason other than happenstance,
If one appears to his lover untrue.
And how quickly do lovers' hearts harden,
When one of the other doth appall,
Like iron statues in a moon garden,
Upon which rain like bitter tears doth fall.
But, a lover's heart is not born of stone,
It is as delicate as porcelaine
And no matter how one attempts to atone,
Once shattered cannot be restored again.
Alas, lovers' goodbyes last forever,
For when "c'est fini!" it is over.

Gone is the sun
Just as a daystar that has flickered away
And like the sun
Your love has gone away.

Now in darkness I'm alone
My romance no longer where you are
Dreaming of a universe unknown
Since my heart is now a dead star.

As I lie awake
My mind spins a carousel
Past amorousness.

In three-quarter view
The true windows of their souls
The eyes of women.

'Twas crossing San Marco's Piazza
Arm in arm against the unmarried wind,
Dodging puddles from the "acqua alta",
When our romantic love did begin.
As dark Moors their bells did chime
Ringing out the early morning hour,
Young and old to mark the passage of time,
A wing'd lion roar'd 'neath the tower.
By the piazzetta to the lagoon,
With its Doge Palace so sublime,
We felt true love under a mystic moon,
While seemingly lost in another time.
And my mask did cast a Venetian glow,
When you whispered "Io te amo".

In a winter's Trieste au Boire,
Wandering where and how
you are.
Having carried these feelings
ever so far,
It may be time to wish on a
star.

Paradigm of love
Sweet and ever unfolding
Thief of summer's light.

Favourite season?
I'm a man for all seasons!
But, when in love, spring!

Praise be to all who wait
For feasts of joy or a soul mate.
Praise be to all who act
On nature's instincts or in
matters abstract.
Neither patience nor action
should be disregarded
For they are not destined for
the fainthearted.

How will I survive
Without the spring in her smile
Autumn on her cheek?

The church bells rang out
Their hearts united as one
As rain fell like rice.

Like kiting through space on a spider's web,
As if migrating to some foreign land,
'Neath the sun, the moon and stars overhead-
'Tis a voyage I don't quite understand.
"To where?" and "How far?" Tis up to the wind,
Landing in the ocean or on the shore,
So like penance for those who've sinned,
Or ultimate reward to those due more.
And on this journey destiny prevails,
With no assurance of a kindly fate
And heartache if the adventure fails:
"O, the chances one takes to find a mate!"
An arduous quest not for the meek,
But the courageous who love do seek.

As the sun fades out of sight
Without a prayer to mark
the end of day
I bow my head and instead
Greet the onset of the night
Where thoughts of you grow
Midst the stars and the moonglow.

In the afterglow,
Old loves faded in the past
Reignite in stars.

After all these years,
Alone in quiet darkness
I still dance with you.

"True love" travels like the wind
Never seen and without passport
Given only to those so destined
An enigma constant to an open heart.

If I think of you,
Are you thinking of me too?
I can't stop sneezing.

His beloved passed
With grief inconsolable
Wrote sonnets sublime.

Gleaming with lovelight
Snow brushing against our cheeks
Walking the road home.

Divergent characters don't we
know -
The famous painter and his bro.

Yet brotherly love hath no greater
show
Than that between Vincent and
young Theo.

And like two sunflowers in a vase,
They now rest side-by-side in
Auvers - Sur - Oise.

Unrequited love
While like a half baked apple
Is better than none.

A rainbow in the mist of summer's light,
Colouring landscapes in my view so gay
And starlight in the heart of winter's night,
Guiding me along my troublesome way,
A child of mother nature she was made,
In harmony with body and spirit
And closer to me than colour to jade,
As the fates deemed her love I did merit.
And when the rich colours began to fade
And the glittering light began to dim,
Romantic love the paradigm she'd made,
As the heroine in a cupid's hymn.
In matters of the heart, 'tis just to say:
That of lovers all, she was "A Per Se!"

Falling in love can be a painful
distraction
But, 'tis so hard to deny this
mysterious attraction.
What is it in you that I so adore
And wish that I had many hearts to
love you more?

In love, we are one another
And our dreams are of each other.
Was there acquiescence from above
That we should be so in love?

When I speak of them
I am lost for words and weep
They are my children!

A red rose was wilting "in extremis"
When a butterfly fluttered with a kiss.
Like a silk angel perched on a deathbed,
For soon the rose was lovely dead.

> Your heart is a diamond
> Set in a platinum ring
> Of my devotion.

My head spinning like a dreidel
I lay unconscious in "the cradle"
Overwhelmed by sublime beauty
I fainted in aesthetic ecstasy
The last moment I recall
Was David standing
contrapposto in the hall.

I sought lust in the shadows of moonlight
On youthful instincts I could not resist
And on this errant journey did loose sight
Of stars in the wake when lovers kissed.
When, on reckless travels to distant lands
With thrills of romance that did not last,
Hard lessons were learned on hot sifting sands
That another lifestyle was to be wished.

    The reds and greens are gone at last
    Where heartaches reemerge from the past
    And loneliness, the minds bell ringer,
    And sadness in the voice of a carol singer.

    Precious memories
    Fill one with profound yearning
    So sweet, so cruel.

A paradigm of eccentricity
He excited all when he played
A genius In technique and tonality
Whose life was anything but stayed.
A man so disconsolate
He often performed through pain
Once paid with butter and chocolate
He was known to the man in the lane.
An icon of his art
And a legend though tragic
He played from his broken heart
And was known as "the last romantic".

Thieves of day's sunlight
Sweet scented growths unfolding
Messengers of love.

How so the north wind doth fatefully blow
When complying with nature's destiny
And Boreus screams that each might know
His cold mystic force rages endlessly.
And yet, thy breath is warm and softly tame,
When you so lovingly whisper my name.

    Ever in search of elusive love
    Like a butterfly the milkweed blossom
    Riding the winds high above
    On a seasonal journey not forgotten.

        At the piano
        Pencil from mouth to soundboard
        Inspired by moonlight
        And a broken heart.

Will my love for thee
Outlive the life of me?
Will your love for me
Outlive the life of thee?
When will it be
That I will know what
will be?
Must I wait for eternity
Before this mystery is
explained to me?

I look into your sad eyes
As we say our goodbyes.
Our tender kiss
Fills me with bliss.
As loving as can be,
I feel like "crying happy"!

There's no justice in the Court of Romance,
Which is governed by the Rules of Love,
As the parties are always biased
And the truth lies with Hora up-above.
The judgements are never astute,
With Cupid's jurisprudence in support,
Since the facts are always in dispute,
All decisions are appealed to the heart.
When sentencing at last is carried out,
On precedents for sim'lar offences,
Of gross injustice there is no doubt:
"In this court, one takes one's chances!"
But, the punishment is never amiss
And retribution is made with a kiss.

'Tis a drug like no other
This passionate love for another
So profoundly rare and tender
A love that lasts forever
While loving is a common occurrence
The truest happens only once.

I heard the swish of snowflakes
As they began falling in the night.
Their melodic voices in a winter's refrain
Seemed to whisper your name
As if they were one with my heart.
Then pianissimo all went silent
As aurora fan-danced beneath the stars.

In her culture I was "un etranger"
And though between us few words were spoken,
Surprisingly, I fell in love with her
And the silence between us was broken.
Our looks of longing and fascination
Which were e'er so innocent and discreet,
Yet, could not disguise our youthful passion,
Nor the tender sighs that were so sweet.
But, all too soon, the ship's whistle blew
And, with promises to write, we parted
As I was off to explore places anew,
Though now love-forlorned and so sad-hearted.
Love travels like the wind with no passport,
E'er greeted warmly by an open heart.

When you joyfully danced 'round that puddle
My instincts alerted me to trouble
As my heart became arhythmic
Watching you with your smile so beatific.
My emotions ran unchecked
Yours was a scene Renoiresque
And I became enchanted in the drizzle
When I heard your girlish giggle.

Meeting Thanatos
He repeated a lament
"Never have I loved!"

Her warm scarlet lips
Moistened by mist and rose dew
Waited to be kissed.

When I think of her
I am without words and grieve
She was my life's love.

Alas, how can it be?
I loved her so much and she not me.
What was it in her I did not see?
Was it just a lovers' mystery?
Surely, it had nothing to do with me
When she pleaded she wanted to be
free.

As I hold your gaze
I taste love on your warm lips
Known pleasures await.

Nocturnal migrants silently in flight
Heard overhead but out of sight
Whether guided by magnetic fields or stars
They always know where they are.
And when I find myself afar
I follow my heart to where you are.
Homeing back to be with thee
No matter how far the distance be.

In the depths of sleep
Shoals of familiar lovers
Upstream in my dreams.

In the leaves a love
Recognized from long ago
Now gone in the wind.

Ex chrysalis spurts a "dash of colour"
The elongated neck of a lover
Created with disdain and disorder
Sensuous nudes cherished the world over.
Defying any classification
And indifferent to avant garde art
Never a slave to his reputation
He painted with an ever valiant heart.
But for him tragedy was no stranger
Struggling with his illness and addiction
There were many lives he put in danger
And informed an early death's prediction.
Dying with his pregnant love by his side
Heartbroken she committed suicide.

As a force of natural selection
Your beauty is a matter of evolution
Causing a rush of "Darwinian" suitors
And attracting unwanted predators.
I am bruised and beset by competing rivals
Performing challenging recitals.
Is there nothing we can do
To prove to all our love is true?

> Running before the wind
> With spinnakers and gull-wings set
> The Calimas advance oil laden gulets
> To the Garden of the Hesperides,
> The three nymphs of evening
> And the golden light of sunsets.

As a rose bud in the womb of
summer's light
And as a new star in the breast of
winter's night
Maternal love the paradigm she made
Close to me as colour to jade.
When the petals began to fall
And the star began to fade,
Her grace and dignity surpassed all.
Loved dearly to this day
For of mothers, she was "A Per Se!

      Winter early nights
      And sunsets in tangerine
      Lovers wait the spring.

She was the model of elegance -
And caused my awkward hesitance.
But the kind fates intervened
And I was at once redeemed.
Our hearts now combined as one -
Our life together just begun.

Were I to sow a nocturnal kiss
Would I reap your diurnall love?
Or would you condemn me to the liss
As I cursed the "blinking" stars above?

    A butterfly kiss
    Dries tears and comforts children
    Honours the milk weed.

I, so like the migrating butterfly,
Was thus determined to capture your heart
And savour your love before I should die
Lest I be unfulfilled there I depart.
Three lifetimes, I have waited for thee,
Midst heartfelt anguish and need,
Tossed by high winds to my destiny,
Then duped by the mimicking milkweed.
But, Hera sprang a branch on which to lite
And savour the warmth of your affection,
After enduring the perils of flight
And the hazards of my long migration.
Alas, love flies on the wings of hope,
Often by stars in one's horoscope.

Born beautiful as the night -
To many females' delight.
As a great romantic poet -
You were the paradigm of heroic.
Never one to assuage,
Your poetry was to your generation a rage.
With an ethical standard considered loose,
You managed to avoid the hangman's noose
(And thy internment in Westminster Abbey
On the grounds of questionable morality).

"Mad, bad and dangerous to Know" -
You were the original "Byronic Hero".
Fleeing to the continent -
Midst rumours of Incest and discontent,
With much prowess to flaunt,
You swam the Hellespont.
While you fought the Turks for their liberty,
The Greeks yielded their hearts to thee
And lovingly entombed yours in Missolonghy.
And now forever renowned -
As by Mother Greece you were crowned.

If love is a neurosis,
Is there a cure?
And if there is a misdiagnosis,
How much pain should one
endure?

And does love begin in Octoberat
noon?
And end in Decemberat
midnight?

And when does love
become obsession?
Is there a definite time
of inception?

Or is it all mere speculation?

Love inspires like rain to wilderness
Giving life to all struggling to survive,
A desert for a prophet's eyes to rest
And an overwrought heart to revive.
One must never shy from love's paradox,
There are places where trees grow out of rocks.

A rare force felt but not understood
Until there is communication with God
Out of heartbreak and despair
So often a curse without care
Flow the arts that transcend
From a mysterious love source
known as "duende".

April rain had cleansed the city of light,
As we s-t-r-o-l-l-e-d along "Rue des Ecoles",
An intimate rendezvous in the night,
Young lovers mated to each other's souls.
Spring often arrives late in Paris,
To Parisians' impatient sighs,
But, unlike the canals of Venice,
It has the sweet air of paradise.
'Tis wonderful to be young and in love -
But in love "au printemps" in Paris,
With the Eiffel Tower soaring above,
Is a lover's fate for each to cherish.
"L'amour de jeunesse sans regret:
La ville lumiere" is a lover's banquet.

Holding her delicate hand
As if she were the child of Mary
Magdelland,
Her Nono cast a noble stare
Then softened his expression
with a prayer:
"Above all, I have so loved thee
But now you must let me be".
Then, with a gentle squeeze,
he turned his lolling head
And moments later he was dead.

Thoughts of you persist
But I know not where you are
Except in my dreams.

Never to kiss your lovely face again
And feel the chill of autumn on your cheek.
"How will I ever endure this pain?"
A lovers' parting is not for the meek.
The emptiness and the disappointment
Have left me in a catatonic state,
I am unable to find contentment,
But, think only on my desperate fate.
O, how I detest such a destiny
That the fates upon me have enacted,
With a sentence of eternal misery
And my tender heart forever fracted.
O, never again will I know such love,
That fit me well as a coo to a dove.

"...Acropolis: Ancient Greek Ruins"
So fraught with questions of our past,
On fallen pillars carved by humans,
Which so like their dynasties did not last.
...Caryatids on the Porch of Maidens
Elegantly supporting the temple roof,
Paid no heed to that which they were laden,
In "contrapposto" from their perch aloof...
On this walk through the ages I wonder'd:
"Will our love last beyond the end of time?"
"Is it as these ruins to be squandered?"
And "Am I a fool thinks it so sublime?"
I pray love's soul lives on in eternity,
Forgive the odd pang of uncertainty.

Roma was as summer sun to the rose
Giving to all life and repose.
Never a gesture to offend,
Be it family member or distant friend.
Always the last to speak,
I can still feel autumn on her cheek.
With a heart full of grace,
She is impossible to replace.

    Loving enigmas
    No matter he, she or it
    Or nothing at all.

    Precious memories
    Fill one with profound yearning
    So sweet, so cruel

I was so young and Luba was so old
But just how old, I was never told.
Her breath a wordsmith might describe
Despite copious nips of apple cider she'd imbibe.
She gently licked salty tears when I wept
And cuddled warmly beside me when I slept.
We were best of friends or so I thought
Like King Arthur and Cavall in Camalot.
But her canine heart belonged to another-
A old stray mongrel and a frequent lover.
They were last seen walking in the morning cold
Just what happened to them, I was never told.

Posing so like a statue in a niche
Enshrouded in a marblesque cloak
Enchantedly, your stare did me bewitch
As burning ambergris bathed you in smoke.
Like a magical symphony in white,
So inviting I did not feel remiss
When, like a thief in the stillness of night,
Invaded your holy purge to steal a kiss.
Tasting your warm lips as I met your eyes
I was possesed by aphrodesia
Though aromata continued to rise
Alas, I was en route to Amoresia.
'Twas like living a lovers' fairytale
All from the regurgence of a whale.

How can it be that I love her so
But she not me?
Is there no equity in love
To ensure reciprocity?
I am in tears with a broken heart
Being slowly torn apart.
Must I endure this painful situation
With no hope of compensation?
Is there no mechanism for redress
Each day, I become more depressed?
Heaven help me! I cannot carry on.
Surely, there is a wise, old Cupid
I can impose on.
But alas, the arrow missed its mark
Now, I wander desperate in the dark.

The Champagne once Chilled,
Stands uncorked beside Crystal
Glasses Unfilled.
And the Long-Stemmed Red
Roses have now Wilted -
For by My Love I have Been Jilted.

The Sweet Amorations have all been
Retracted -
My heart like a Chalice has been fracted.
Jealousy Swept Away her Love like a
Feather -
How could I have been so Enamoured
with her?
And what Sadistic Instincts were at play?
Now my "Lifelove" must wait for a
Brighter Day -
When the Tears and the Heartache have
all Faded Away.

It came from nowhere
When I saw her lovely face
But my heart knew!

I kiss you in dreams
And the night air as though you
And now were you here.

Like the butterfly
Searching the fields for milkweed
Am I, open hearts.

Words are not enough
To hold are what arms are for
I long to hold you!

It was when she spoke my name -
I knew my life would never be the same.
Was it her voice and its vibrance,
Or was it her lovely countenance?
A hand offered in kindness,
Or my own love-blindness?
That I will never know -
It could have been instinctive though.

Enshrouded in dreams
Of a true and lasting love
I wanted to sleep.

They come in the night
Faces and voices of loves
That tear at my heart.

Dear, sweet paternal cousin -
You soothed me with foreign pastorals
That made it seem all so natural.
You comforted me with thy firm breasts,
I was by thee a child blessed.
How insensitive the hands of fate
That claimed thee sooner than late.
Lifeless in thy virginal white wedding dress
And me wanting to caress,
An untouched grief overcame my defences
And to sadness I lost my senses.
Tender memories of thee linger still -
Know they always will!

Our merry carousel waltz has ended
The flying horses no longer go 'roun'
The organ music has long ago faded
For our circus has already left town.
Perhaps I was masquerading
Pretending to be someone I am not
And with commitment always evading
So like the harlequin ...with love forgot.
Now it all seems like such a sideshow
And I don't know how or what to feel
Of those moments of joy and scenes of woe
Like the highs and lows of a Ferris wheel.
Sound as a striker bell true love can be
When not, melts away like cotton candy.

With the bouquet of ripe grapes in the air,
We biked the vineyards of Niagara,
Basking in the harvest sun without care,
Giddy from wine - then "ABRACADABRA!"
With blue skies and white clouds on the wing,
We were thunderstruck as we fell in love,
So happy were we, we began to sing,
As starlings mermurated high above.
Like an ancient mystical symbol,
Mist from "onguiaahra" came into view,
A visual indigenous signal
Proclaiming to the world our love was true.
Our forefathers knew of its magic force,
Wise were we to let nature take its course.

With lips that had recently been kissed
- As few men could resist -
She stood sensuously gazing unfocused
Out-of-the-light as if not to be noticed.
Leaning against a renaissance bureau,
She looked as if she were a maiden in a
chiaroscuro.
With loosened hair that looked so
stunning,
It was hard to imagine she could be so
cunning.

> Snow swirling all 'round
> Kissing winter from her lips
> Fires of passion burn.

As the summer sun glorifies the rose,
Such was the depth of my affection
When I beheld as Michelangelo's
Your beauteous thesbian expression.
The emotion with which you spoke your lines
And the romantic tone of your voice,
I was as if framed in Valentines
And my long-imprisoned heart did rejoice.
Then as the final act concluded
With the loose ends all resolved,
I realized I was deluded
And had become with thee too involved.
Yet, so inspired to feel love in this way
And still be willing to give my heart away.

So unfettered by the love I felt -
Even a cautious heart like mine did melt.
The gifts I gave to be her fave,
As if in irons, I became her slave.
Though at times she seemed delighted,
My love at best was unrequited.
Alas for me, she cared not so much -
Now all that remains are memories
of her scent and her touch.

> Though our love has changed
> In our lifetime together
> It has not perished.

O, such sweet and innocent affection,
As a maiden's kiss blown to a lone doe,
Ne'er did I know such sincere devotion,
Which was delicate as a feather though.
Probing and curious were her fingertips
Rippling across my skin like tide pebbles,
As her lips enticed my moon to eclipse,
Gentle and soft and lush as rose petals.
Her heart, so true and unencumbered,
Was like the refreshing zephyrs of spring
And, as a scholar, I often pondered
On how her love for me meant everything.
By sad fates we're no longer together,
But, true love like this should last forever.

How could she possibly cope
When she had lost her life's hope?
Neither "Heartfelt Sympathies" nor
"Mournful Prayer"
Can diminish the grief of love's despair.
For when love our hearts doth fill,
The anguish of its loss is greater still.

    It only comes once
    The love that outlives starlight
    Once in a lifetime.

    A million kisses
    Burning in the summer sun
    I lavish on you.

In the hurtful denouement of romance,
Love quickly melts away as "cire perdue",
For no reason other than happenstance,
If one appears to his lover untrue.
And how quickly do lovers' hearts harden,
When one of the other doth appall,
Like iron statues in a moon garden,
Upon which rain like bitter tears doth fall.

So enraptured with the Caravaggio,
She stood transposed by his great masterpiece,
As her tears like a spring rindle did flow,
Her tender heart stripped of restful peace.
So profound the depth of her sorrow therein,
She was as one of the loving grieved,
Thus moved by the sad death of the Virgin,
The scene depicted she truly believed
'Tis a gift to feel vicariously,
A true lover's palette obviously.

No elixir for heartache
No matter how hard he tried
He could not forget her.

How could I not love
When you were so loveable?
Am I loveable?

Love is the only colour that I
know
And the most beautiful of the
rainbow.

So innocent and yet so sensuous -
She was the paradigm of naturalness.
With her dress she did not fret -
So like the fashion of Marie Antoinette.
Her skin glowing midst blues and greys,
Enhanced the depth of her enticing gaze.
The curves of her shoulders and breasts
Testified to her beauty blessed.
While me she did enthral,
She was just a tondo on the wall.

O, sweet scented growths ever unfolding
And daring thieves of Hyperion's Light,
Thy fauvist beauty to my love must bring,
In the fullness of day or in lunar's light,
A rainbow's palate her heart to inspire
And open its gate to a loving admirer,
Whose own heart is filled with love and desire
And with passion burns as our star's own fire.
Yet, above all else you must stay sunfast,
Lest the power of your hues will not last
And their message too short will not persist,
Alas, my deep affections she may resist.
But, if in all this you will succeed,
Your life's sacrifice will honour love's deed.

Her eyes like black holes in the universe
Into which my life's energy did flow
A projected astral sorceress curse
Filling my heart with suffering and woe.
A force so profound it captured my sight
And warped the space-time fabric of my soul
And reshaped with empyrean delight
Mind, life and transcendental passions whole.
Then like a comet's death dive to the sun
Her mystic love lost its radiant glow
As legend Icarus's flight undone
Or like "white dwarfs" a billion years ago.
Yet, when I gaze into the sky at night,
Zeus knows I'll love her longer than starlight.

I'm sure it was you
On the wings of a sweet dream
I wanted to stay.

Chalk and brushes flying through the air
The students seemed not to care-
"'Twas something about the sun..."
Falling on deaf ears all but one
Whose love of Shakespeare had just
begun.

A thumping blow
White calla lilies in the window
Blood like a heart
A heavenly message in art.
'Twas late one summer
And a love like no other.